Riding With the Mail

Riding With *the* Mail

The Story of the Pony Express

By Gare Thompson

NATIONAL GEOGRAPHIC

WASHINGTON, D.C.

Founded in 1888, the National Geographic Society is one of the largest nonprofit scientific and educational organizations in the world. It reaches more than 285 million people worldwide each month through its official journal, NATIONAL GEOGRAPHIC, and its four other magazines; the National Geographic Channel; television documentaries; radio programs; films; books; videos and DVDs; maps; and interactive media. National Geographic has funded more than 8,000 scientific research projects and supports an education program combating geographic illiteracy.

For more information, please call
1-800-NGS-LINE (647-5463) or write to the following address:

National Geographic Society
1145 17th Street N.W.
Washington, D.C. 20036-4688
U.S.A.

Visit us online at www.nationalgeographic.com/books

For information about special discounts for bulk purchases, please contact
National Geographic Books Special Sales at ngspecsales@ngs.org

For rights or permissions inquiries, please contact National Geographic
Books Subisidiary Rights: ngbookrights@ngs.org

Copyright © 2007 National Geographic Society

Text revised from *The Story of the Pony Express* in the National Geographic Windows on Literacy program from National Geographic School Publishing, © 2002 National Geographic Society

All rights reserved. Reproduction of the whole or any part of the contents without written permission from the publisher is prohibited.

Published by National Geographic Society. Washington, D.C. 20036

Design by Project Design Company
Photo Editor: Annette Kiesow
Project Editor: Anita Schwartz

Printed in the United States

**Library of Congress
Cataloging-in-Publication Data**

Thompson, Gare.
 Riding with the mail : the story of the pony express / by Gare Thompson.
     p. cm. – (National Geographic history chapters)
  ISBN 978-1-4263-0192-6 (library)
1. Pony express–Juvenile literature.   I. Title.
HE6375.P65T56 2007
383'.1430978–dc22

2007007897

Photo Credits
Front Cover: © National Postal Museum/Smithsonian Institution; Spine, Endpaper: © The Granger Collection, NY; 2-3: © Phil Schermeister/CORBIS; 6, 10, 18, 32: © Getty Images; 8: © Dynamic Graphics/Jupiterimages; 9, 17, 26-27: © St. Joseph Museum, St. Joseph, Missouri; 14: © James L. Amos/National Geographic Image Collection; 15, 19, 21: © Private Collection/ Peter Newark Western Americana/ The Bridgeman Art Library; 16: © Private Collection/ © Look and Learn/ The Bridgeman Art Library; 20, 34: © Library of Congress; 22: © Phil Schermeister/National Geographic Image Collection; 24: © James L. Amos/CORBIS; 25: © Charles E. Rotkin/CORBIS; 28: © Dave G. Houser/CORBIS; 31: © Time Life Pictures/Getty Images; 35: © Pablo San Juan/CORBIS.

Endsheets: Stamps on an envelope that rode the Pony Express in 1861.

Contents

The town of San Francisco, California, grew rapidly as people came west to look for gold. By 1851, about 25,000 people were living there.

Moving West

In the mid-1800s, many people living in the eastern part of the United States moved west to California and Oregon. People moved west for many reasons. Some people wanted to find gold. Others were looking for cheap farmland. By 1860, almost 500,000 people lived west of the Rocky Mountains.

Mail traveled quickly in the eastern half of the country. Trains and the telegraph kept news flowing as far west as the Mississippi River. But mail to the West Coast moved very slowly. There were no telegraph lines yet west of the Mississippi, so you could not send a telegram.

In the early 1800s, the Post Office Department bought a number of stagecoaches to deliver the mail over some of the country's better post roads.

Mail traveled to the West Coast by stagecoach. These trips took a long time. Stagecoaches did not go directly from the East Coast to the West Coast. They did not travel in straight lines. They traveled from town to town. Towns were far apart. Often, the stagecoaches were delayed by bad weather. It could take a month or more for a letter sent from the East Coast to reach the West Coast.

One of the most popular mail routes from New York to California was by sea. Steamships carried mail from New York across the sea to Panama. Wagons, mules, or stagecoaches carried the mail across Panama. Then the mail was loaded onto a second ship that sailed to California.

This route could take more than a month. People did not want to wait that long for their mail. They wanted to hear news quickly. Someone had to come up with a faster way to get mail to and from the West Coast.

In the mid-1800s, steam-powered trains traveling at 15 miles (24 kilometers) per hour carried mail in the eastern part of the United States.

PONY EXPRESS!

CHANGE OF TIME!

REDUCED RATES!

10 Days to San Francisco!

LETTERS

WILL BE RECEIVED AT THE

OFFICE, 84 BROADWAY,

NEW YORK,

Up to 4 P. M. every TUESDAY,

and

Up to 2½ P. M. every SATURDAY,

Which will be forwarded to connect with the PONY EXPRESS leaving ST. JOSEPH, Missouri,

Every WEDNESDAY and SATURDAY at 11 P. M.

TELEGRAMS

Sent to Fort Kearney on the mornings of MONDAY and FRIDAY, will connect with PONY leaving St. Joseph, WEDNESDAYS and SATURDAYS.

EXPRESS CHARGES.

LETTERS weighing half ounce or under $1 00
For every additional half ounce or fraction of an ounce 1 00
In all cases to be enclosed in 10 cent Government Stamped Envelopes,
And all Express CHARGES Pre-paid.

☞ PONY EXPRESS ENVELOPES For Sale at our Office.

WELLS, FARGO & CO., Ag'ts.

Chapter 1

Make Way for the Pony Express

William Russell had a large freight and stagecoach company. A senator from California asked Russell and his company to build a mail route from St. Joseph, Missouri, to Sacramento, California. St. Joseph was as far west as the railroad went and the telegraph reached.

Many people believed that such an overland route could not be built. Most of the land between Missouri and California was unexplored by most whites. Native Americans lived on the lands.

◀ Wells Fargo advertised how fast the new Pony Express service would deliver letters and telegrams to the West Coast.

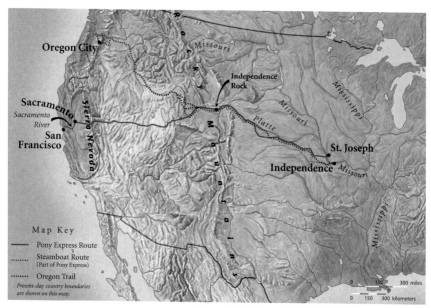

The Pony Express route ran through parts of what are now Missouri, Kansas, Nebraska, Colorado, Wyoming, Utah, Nevada, and California.

William Russell believed that it was possible to build a year-round overland mail route to the West. He formed a company to create a fast mail delivery service. It was called the Pony Express. Russell promised that the Pony Express would deliver mail to the West Coast in just ten days!

Russell and his company set to work. Starting early in 1860, he built a mail route across almost 2,000 miles (3,200 kilometers). The first part of the route followed the Oregon Trail. Settlers had used this trail to travel west from Missouri to California and Oregon. It was the fastest and most direct route to the West Coast.

Russell set up a system that worked like a relay race. One Pony Express rider would start the trip at St. Joseph, Missouri. Other riders would continue the trip, riding day and night. They would ride in all kinds of weather. They would ride across plains, mountains, and deserts. Then, the last rider in the relay would arrive in Sacramento, California, with the mail ten days later.

Did You Know?

Russell's company built about 190 Pony Express stations. Riders changed horses at each station. That way the rider was always riding a rested horse.

Pony Express stations, such as the one shown here, were about 10 to 15 miles (15 to 25 kilometers) apart.

A rider ended his ride when he reached a home station. There another rider waited to take his place. When the tired rider reached a home station, he threw his mailbag over a fresh horse. A new rider leaped onto the horse and raced off.

Russell's company bought more than 400 fast horses. They hired hundreds of men and women to work in the stations. They advertised in newspapers for riders.

Did You Know?

Most of the Pony Express stations were simple cabins. One station, Lodge Pole Creek, was a large hole dug in the side of a hill.

The Riders

Pony Express riders had to be expert riders. They had to know how to handle horses. They had to be brave and honest. They had to promise not to swear or get into fights. And they had to want to deliver the mail on time.

The riders earned $100 per month. They ranged in age from 11 years to 45 years. They all had one goal—to ride as fast as they could. They were ready to do whatever it took to make sure the mail made it safely to California in ten days.

Billy Richardson, Johnny Frye (standing) and Charles Cliff and Gus Cliff (seated) rode for the Pony Express.

Pony Express riders ranged in age from 11 to 45.

Each rider rode 75 to 100 miles (120–160 kilometers) a day. He changed horses every 10 to 15 miles (15–25 kilometers). A rider could change horses in about two minutes. Most riders rode about 10 miles (about 16 kilometers) per hour.

Meet "Bronco Charlie"

The youngest Pony Express rider was "Bronco Charlie." He was only 11 years old when he rode for the Pony Express. He replaced a rider who had been attacked by Native Americans. Before the stationkeepers could stop him, Charlie was on his horse and riding off with the mail. He rode for the Pony Express for five months until it closed.

Seventy years later, in 1931, Charlie rode his horse cross-country. He delivered mail from the mayor of New York City to the mayor of San Francisco. It took him seven months! He was 81 years old when he did it. He made the trip in honor of the 70th anniversary of the Pony Express. He is the only man ever to have ridden his horse cross-country alone to deliver the mail.

The Route

The Pony Express route was long. But that was not the only problem. The route was also dangerous. The riders traveled alone across land that was largely unexplored and unpopulated. They rode through burning hot deserts and across wild, roaring rivers. They climbed steep, rocky mountains.

Riders traveled across rugged land and mountainous trails.

Pony Express horses had to be fast and hardy enough to ride through driving rains, ice, and snowstorms.

Riders could not stop for bad weather. The mail had to get through. It had to be delivered on time. Riders had to travel through all kinds of weather, including blizzards and thunderstorms.

Riders had to guard against wolves and other wild animals. They were also on the lookout for Native Americans who might attack them or any of the relay stations.

By the 1860s, trains were delivering mail to towns and cities between the East Coast and the Midwest.

Chapter 2

The First Ride

The Pony Express began service from St. Joseph, Missouri, on April 3, 1860. The train bringing the mail from the East Coast was late. But when people heard the train whistle, they knew the mail was nearly there. When the mail finally arrived, the rider threw the mailbag over the saddle and leaped onto his horse. The crowd cheered. The rider set out on his long, hard journey.

Riders carried the mail in a saddlebag called a *mochila.*

Riders traveled through Mitchell Pass in what is today Nebraska.

First, he had to cross the Missouri River. Luckily, there was a paddleboat to take him across. Then he rode through barren countryside until he reached the first home station. Worn out, the first rider jumped off his horse. He had ridden almost 100 miles (160 kilometers)!

The next rider rode across the flat land in the center of the country. He raced through the valley of the Platte River and headed northwest to the next home station. There, another rider waited.

The next few riders rode through the part of the country that is now Nebraska. The hot, dry land slowly rose toward the Rocky Mountains. There were almost no trees. The land was covered with tough prairie grass.

At each home station the mail was passed to a new rider. As the riders continued moving west the land became more and more rugged. By the time a rider reached Independence Rock in what is now Wyoming, the mail still had a long way to go. It had only traveled about half the distance to Sacramento, California.

Did You Know?

The letters that the Pony Express riders carried were written on lightweight paper. The letters were wrapped in oiled silk cloth to protect the paper from being damaged in bad weather.

From Independence Rock, the riders made their way through the Rocky Mountains. These mountains were steep. The trail was narrow and rocky. But the worst was yet to come.

Many settlers going west carved their names and the date of their journey into Independence Rock.

Riders faced a difficult and dangerous route through the Rocky Mountains.

Just past the mountains was a vast desert. As the riders crossed the long stretch of desert, the sun beat down. Dust storms swirled. The riders who crossed the desert grew tired, hot, and thirsty. Yet, they kept on going to deliver the mail on time.

The next riders faced even more dangers. They had to make it through the Sierra Nevada. Riders rode up steep mountain passes and through narrow canyons. They faced howling winds, icy rain, and blinding snowstorms.

Finally, the last rider arrived in Sacramento on April 13, 1860. The town went wild with excitement. Bands played. People cheered and waved flags. The rider delivered more than 80 letters. When the cheering stopped, the rider boarded the steamboat that would take him to San Francisco. He still had letters for people there.

People living in San Francisco cheered when the last rider arrived from Sacramento by steamship with the mail.

The steamboat arrived in San Francisco at midnight. It seemed as if the whole town was there to greet the rider. San Francisco no longer seemed quite so far away from the rest of the country. Mail had arrived in just ten days! William Russell was right. His Pony Express could deliver the mail to the West Coast faster than it had ever been delivered.

THE
PONY EXPRESS

THE PONY EXPRESS
St. Joseph, Missouri

A statue in St. Joseph, Missouri,
honors the brave Pony Express riders.

Chapter 3

The End of the Pony Express

The Pony Express lasted just 18 months. The riders made 308 complete runs. They rode a total of 616,000 miles (991,760 kilometers). They delivered almost 35,000 letters. And the Pony Express riders lost only one mailbag!

The fastest delivery time was 7 days and 17 hours. That was in March 1861, when Abraham Lincoln was sworn in as president. At his swearing in, the president delivered a speech called an inaugural address. Afterwards, Pony Express riders carried a copy of Lincoln's speech from St. Joseph to Sacramento.

William Russell's company lost money, but it was the telegraph that really ended the Pony Express. Samuel Morse invented the telegraph in 1843. By the 1860s, there were telegraph offices in every major city. Western Union completed the first transcontinental telegraph line on October 24, 1861. People could send messages across the country faster than any rider could deliver mail.

People did not forget the Pony Express riders. Many people thought they were heroes. People wrote letters to newspapers thanking the riders for their courage.

Did You Know?

The spirit of the Pony Express lives on in the unofficial motto of today's mail carriers. Inscribed on New York City's General Post Office building are these words: "Neither snow nor rain nor heat nor gloom of night stays these couriers from the swift completion of their appointed rounds."

Workers raise transcontinental telegraph lines,
marking the end to the Pony Express.

Fast, Faster, Fastest

Even before the Pony Express, trains were delivering the mail. In 1869, the first U.S. transcontinental railroad was built. Mail could be delivered by rail from coast to coast. More railroads were built. By 1930, 10,000 trains were moving mail into every city, town, and village in the country.

Airmail came next. In 1918, the U.S. Postal Service took to the skies. The first route was between Washington, D.C., and New York, with a stop in between in Philadelphia.

◀ The U.S. Postal Service delivers about 20 billion letters, cards, and packages between Thanksgiving and Christmas.

Today, the U.S. Postal Service uses almost every kind of transportation. That includes boats, bicycles, and even mules. It delivers mail to every house and business no matter how far. That's more than 200 billion pieces of mail every year. Some of this mail is express mail, delivered in just one day.

By 1858, there were mailboxes on the streets in large cities.

Did You Know?

In 1959, a guided missile transported 3,000 pieces of mail from the Navy submarine USS *Barbero* to a Navy air station in Florida.

A mail carrier crosses the river to deliver mail to the Havasupai Reservation in Arizona.

The hardest mail route in the U.S. has to be the one that goes deep down into the Grand Canyon. That's where 600 Havasupai Indians live. Five days a week, a mule train travels six to eight hours to deliver their mail.

Today, the fastest way to send a message is by electronic mail, or e-mail. E-mail became popular in the 1990s. It's the mail delivery service many of us use every day.

From horseback to airmail to e-mail, mail service keeps getting faster and faster. What will come next?

How to Write an A+ Report

1. Choose a topic.
- Find something that interests you.
- Make sure it is not too big or too small.

2. Find sources.
- Ask your librarian for help.
- Use many different sources: books, magazine articles, and Web sites.

3. Gather information.
- Take notes. Write down the big ideas and interesting details.
- Use your own words.

4. Organize information.
- Sort your notes into groups that make sense.

- Make an outline. Put your groups of notes in the order you want to write your report.

5. Write your report.

- Write an introduction that tells what the report is about.

- Use your outline and notes as you write to make sure you say everything you want to say in the order you want to say it.

- Write an ending that tells about your report.

- Write a title.

6. Revise and edit your report.

- Read your report to make sure it makes sense.

- Read it again to check spelling, punctuation, and grammar.

7. Hand in your report!

Glossary

blizzard   severe snowstorm

canyon   deep valley with steep sides

electronic mail (e-mail)   mail or messages sent by computers

relay race   a race in which one person passes something to another person, such as one Pony Express rider passing the mail to another Pony Express rider

route   a set path or line of travel

stagecoach   a carriage pulled by horses to carry people or mail

telegram   a message sent and received with a telegraph

telegraph   a device for sending and receiving coded messages over wires across long distances

transcontinental   crossing the continent, such as telegraph lines that crossed North America from New York, on the East Coast, to California, on the West Coast

Further Reading

• Books •

Anderson, Peter. *The Pony Express* (Cornerstones of Freedom). New York: Children's Press, 1996. Grades 4–6, 32 pages.

Brill, Marlene Targ. *Bronco Charlie and the Pony Express* (On My Own History). Minneapolis, MN: Carolrhoda Books, 2004. Grades 1–3, 48 pages.

Fuchs, Bernie. *Ride Like the Wind: A Tale of the Pony Express.* New York: Scholastic/Blue Sky Press, 2004. Grades 1–4, 32 pages.

Harness, Cheryl. *They're Off! The Story of the Pony Express.* New York: Aladdin, 2002. Grades 3–5, 32 pages.

Kroll, Steven. *Pony Express!* New York: Scholastic, 1996. Grades 3–6, 40 pages.

• Web Sites •

National Park Service
www.nps.gov/poex/

Pony Express Museum
www.ponyexpress.org/

Pony Express Home Station
www.xphomestation.com

The St. Joseph Museums
www.stjosephmuseum.org/
PonyExpress/history.html

U.S. Postal Service
www.usps.com/postalhistory/

Index